Shark Encounters

Michael Patrick O'Neill
Batfish Books

O'Neill, Michael Patrick
Shark Encounters / Michael Patrick O'Neill
ISBN 978-0-9728653-4-0
Library of Congress Control Number: 2007904078

Printed in China

Batfish Books
PO Box 32909
Palm Beach Gardens, FL 33420-2909
www.batfishbooks.com

Photographer's Website:
www.mpostock.com

10 9 8 7 6 5 4 3 2

CONTENTS

Silvertips (*Carcharhinus albimarginatus*); French Polynesia

Sand Tiger (*Carcharias taurus*); North Carolina

Introduction

SHARK!

No word in the English language triggers such a powerful reaction. When we hear it, our hearts beat faster and our adrenaline pumps harder. If we are in the water, our feet move faster to get us out as quickly as possible. Or at least faster than the next guy.

It's only natural we behave this way. After all, our DNA tells us to flee, and to boot, our culture continually reinforces the stereotypical and inaccurate image of the shark as a villain cruising the breakers in search of the next human meal.

Fortunately, the perception and reality of these spectacular creatures are completely different, and the true portrait of the animal is gradually emerging from the murk.

In *Shark Encounters*, sequel to *Let's Explore Sharks*, we'll learn in depth about a whole new group of sharks, from the notorious Bull to the elegant Silvertip. We will also appreciate the critical role they play in the marine environment and why they urgently need our help to ensure their long-term survival.

The Intimidator

Experts rank the Bull shark (*Carcharhinus leucas*) as the most dangerous, even more so than the Great White or Tiger. For the most part, these two other species favor ecosystems where relatively few people venture: cold, remote coastlines in the Pacific, Atlantic and Indian Oceans, and distant offshore zones.

On the other hand, the Bull likes to hunt where we like to swim: beaches, inlets, coral reefs, lagoons and even freshwater rivers such as the Mississippi, Amazon and Ganges. Named for its aggressive nature, this impressive predator reaches 12 ft. in length, weighs over 500 lbs. and lives in tropical waters worldwide.

Its diet includes fish, other sharks, turtles, dolphins and even animals that get carried away from land by currents and rivers.

Unpredictable and territorial, the Bull shark on occasion runs into trouble with people. Its vicious reputation is legendary, and surfers, villagers, swimmers and fishermen have learned to enjoy the ocean all the while keeping an eye out for potential danger.

While most encounters with Bulls are rare, accidental and unplanned, a few are intentional.

There is a special place in the South Pacific where scuba divers actively seek out these sharks to admire them safely up close.

Due to its worldwide distribution, the Bull is known by several names, including Zambezi shark in South Africa and Ganges shark in India.

Yanuca Island

Welcome to Beqa Lagoon, Fiji Islands.

Described as an underwater Eden, this pristine lagoon contains some of the richest reefs on the planet.

Against this backdrop of ultra-clear water and lush soft corals, adventurers experience one of the most thrilling dives of their lives.

At Shark Reef, a special site in the lagoon, divemasters hand-feed Bull sharks, and tourists can "rub elbows" with the much-maligned hunters, ultimately realizing these great carnivores are not bloodthirsty killers.

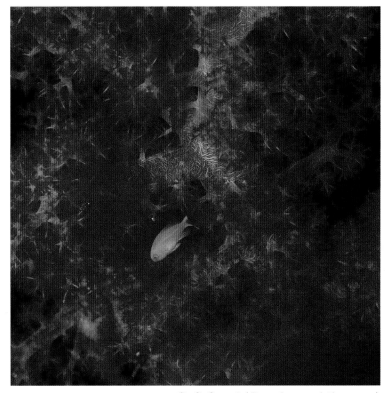

Soft Coral (*Dendronephthya sp.*)

Big Mamma in action. Physical characteristics of Bulls include a heavy-set body, small eyes and a large, first dorsal fin.

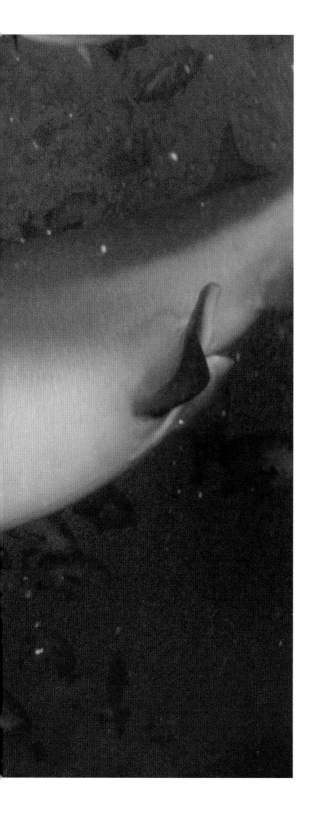

Instead, the sharks line up and take turns eating a favorite snack – tuna heads.

Big Mamma, the largest in the family, is the first in line, followed by her smaller companions. It is not unusual for them to devour over 300 lbs. of fish scraps during the dive, and once full, they leave and show absolutely no interest in the divers.

Shark dives are highly controversial. Some people are against them, claiming feeding changes the sharks' behavior and makes them associate humans with food. In disagreement, others believe there are positive aspects to them.

In Beqa, for instance, they take place on an inaccessible reef and raise money so local villagers can build schools and health clinics for their children.

The Ultimate Shark

The Scalloped Hammerhead (*Sphyrna lewini*) is one of the largest types of Hammerhead sharks, growing to 12 ft. in length and inhabiting many ecosystems, from shallow estuaries to deep, offshore waters. Despite its primitive appearance, it's among the most advanced of all sharks, armed with ultra-keen sight and smell, thanks in part to its elongated, electroreceptor-filled head.

Although found worldwide, Scalloped Hammerheads are known as the "ambassadors" of Cocos Island, a far-flung outpost 340 miles offshore Costa Rica in the Eastern Pacific. This green pin-drop in the middle of nowhere is the definition of remote; access is limited to expedition vessels that take over 30 hours to make the trip. Once there, travelers are greeted by an eerie isolation, for it's the largest uninhabited island in the world.

The waters surrounding it are full of life and can be compared to Africa's Serengeti plains and Brazil's Amazon jungle.

Underwater predators and prey of all kinds polish their survival skills in front of intrepid divers, who endure one of the bumpiest boat rides around to witness firsthand one of nature's greatest spectacles.

Cocos remains shark infested – for now. Squadrons of Scalloped Hammerheads still haunt seamounts (underwater mountains) like Alcyone, a dive site discovered by explorer Jacques Cousteau in 1987.

Scientists believe the earth's magnetic field may guide the sharks to the seamounts during the day, where they socialize and relax.

Like many large sharks, Scalloped Hammerheads are threatened from overfishing.

While common in Cocos and other Eastern Pacific islands like the Galapagos (Ecuador) and Malpelo (Colombia), the species has been hit really hard in other locations.

Off the east coast of the United States, for example, the numbers of Scalloped Hammerheads are down by an estimated 97%! Simply put, fishermen have wiped out this species in the area, and the absence of the Scalloped Hammerhead and other large sharks disrupts the natural balance of the environment.

Cow Nose rays, a favorite prey of these sharks, eat enormous amounts of scallops, oysters and clams. Now, without the sharks, the rays are destroying scallop fisheries, particularly in North Carolina.

The Night Stalker

While the major draw for divers in Cocos is the Scalloped Hammerhead, the Whitetip Reef (*Triaenodon obesus*) is the most abundant. During the day, thousands of these sleek, cat-like sharks loiter around the island's volcanic ledges and pinnacles. Many crowd caves and cracks in the rocks, sleeping like logs, patiently waiting for nightfall.

When the sun sets, they are transformed. Fully alert, they search for small fish hidden in the reef. Oftentimes, they follow a Black Jack (*Caranx lugubris*), another talented nocturnal hunter. Like a hunting dog, the Black Jack flushes the target out from cover and a knock-down-drag-out melee ensues.

If the doomed fish tucks inside a hole lined with razor-sharp coral, it's no problem for the Whitetips.

They sport extra-thick skin and protective eye ridges – perfect adaptations for this type of roughhousing. When the attack is over, there is nothing left but a cloud of sand and debris. The group then moves on to find its next victim.

By the way, the temporary alliance between unrelated fish like the Black Jack and the Whitetips is relatively common, as different animals will often cooperate to eat or protect themselves.

One of the most common reef sharks, Whitetips live throughout the Pacific and Indian Oceans, including the Red Sea. They can reach 7 ft. but are usually much smaller.

This shark is distinguishable by its blunt head and the white markings on both the first dorsal fin and tip of the tail.

What's on the White-tips' Menu?

At night, no small fish is safe. For Whitetips in Cocos, the evening's dinner specials may include *clockwise from top left*: Mexican Hogfish (*Bodianus diplotaenia*), Blue and Gold Snappers (*Lutjanus viridis*), Snowflake Moray (*Echidna nebulosa*) and juvenile Sailfin Grouper (*Mycteroperca olfax*).

Meet the expert: the Black Jack is strong, cunning and capable of finding reef fish holed up in the rocks.

For generations, fortune hunters flocked to Cocos in search of buried treasure, hidden years ago by pirates. After more than 300 failed expeditions, speculators and the Costa Rican government – custodian of the island – realized the real treasure of Cocos was the incredible profusion of wildlife swimming below its turbulent waters. A national park since 1992, it will hopefully remain a refuge for sharks forever.

The Majesty of the Seas

Few would argue that the Silvertip (*Carcharhinus albimarginatus*) is the most beautiful of all sharks. A masterpiece of design, it's flawless. Think of it as a missile with fins and teeth that is always on the lookout for a meal. Growing to 11 ft., it's the largest of the reef sharks and calls the entire tropical Indo-Pacific region home – from eastern Africa to the western coast of Central America.

This wide-ranging shark is viviparous, that is, it gives birth to live young. Females bear fewer than 11 pups after a gestation period that lasts up to one year. When born, the babies are from 25 to 36 inches long and perfect replicas of their parents.

Safeguarding large, pregnant females like this one is crucial to the species' long-term survival.

The limited number of offspring produced by large sharks such as Silvertips makes them particularly vulnerable to overexploitation. There is no way their population can remain stable with the amount of commercial fishing going on today.

This species' Latin name (*albimarginatus*) tells us a little bit about its appearance. The first part of the word – *albi* – means *white*, while the second half – *marginatus* – signifies *to surround with an edge or boundary*.

A scientific name often illustrates an animal's physical characteristics. In the Silvertip's case, it describes the coloration of the fins and tail.

Silvertips can be found from the ocean's surface all the way down to 2,500 ft. in depth.

Shadowed by Big-Eye Trevally (*Caranx sexfasciatus*), a Silvertip patrols Avatoru Pass in Rangiroa. Situated in French Polynesia in the South Pacific, Rangiroa is an enormous coral island known for its prolific marine life. Fish, dolphins, turtles, manta rays and sharks stack up in the pass in jaw-dropping numbers that leave novice and veteran divers awestruck.

Examples of fish found there include *clockwise from left*: Napoleon Wrasse (*Cheilinus undulates*), Bohar Snapper (*Lutjanus bohar*) and Butterflyfish (*Chaetodon sp.*).

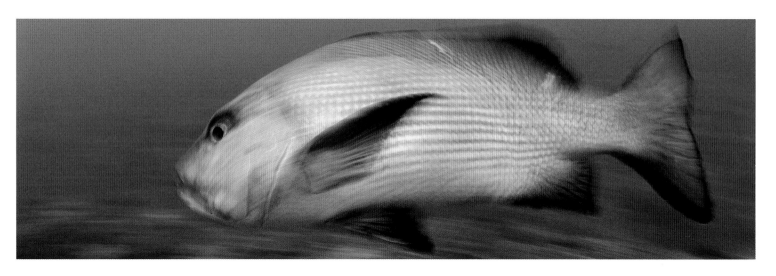

The "Gangster" Shark

The highly aggressive Grey Reef shark (*Carcharhinus amblyrhynchos*) is not bashful at all, confidently approaching divers and often bumping and biting everything in its path while feeding. In fact, during a frenzy the shark will even tear into camera equipment and other inedible objects with as much gusto as if it were eating a grouper fillet!

One reason why Grey Reefs behave this way lies in their social structure. Living in large packs, individuals must be extremely competitive to catch food before their colleagues, and as a result, they are always ready to strike. They savor ornamental reef fish, lobster, octopi and even the young of their own species.

When provoked or cornered, this territorial shark will perform an impressive threat display alerting trespassers, including divers, to stay away. It will arch its back and lower its pectoral fins, swimming back and forth in the same place.

If these warnings are ignored, there's a good chance it will launch an almost indefensible attack that can result in significant injury.

The Grey Reef will try to bite and drive the intruder away from its personal space with such unbelievable ferocity that it makes a Tiger shark look like a puppy.

Reaching a maximum of 7 ft. in length, this Pacific Ocean shark can easily be identified by the black ridge running along the edge of its tail.

A professional filmmaker carefully negotiates his way around Grey Reefs while documenting their feeding behavior. Around sharks, it pays to move very calmly to avoid attracting their attention.

The best place in the world to see this species is French Polynesia, where the locals call it "Raira."

A Shadow in the Shallows

The Blacktip Reef (*Carcharhinus melanopterus*) is the terror of tropical fish that live in protected lagoons in the Pacific and Indian Oceans. This small shark enters ultra-shallow water – usually during the incoming tide – to ambush baitfish, crabs, squid and even sea snakes, which, in northern Australia, account for 25% of this species' diet.

There are many sharks informally known as "blacktips," but the Blacktip Reef is unmistakable from the others because of its small size and very pronounced black markings on the fins and tail. The two dorsal fins also have a whitish band immediately below the black markings.

Blacktip Reefs are one of the few shark species that hunts in small groups.

Like most sharks, the Blacktip Reef has a darker back than stomach. Scientists call this *countershading,* and it's ideal camouflage. Seen from the top, the shark is hard to see against the reef, and from the bottom, almost impossible because of the sun.

Growing to no more than 5 ft., this beautiful little hunter must also be on guard, for big Hammerheads, Bulls and Tigers will try to eat it if it strays too far from the protection of sandbars and coral.

Given its attractive coloration, mild disposition and hardiness, the Blacktip Reef is a popular aquarium exhibit, adapting well and even breeding and having young in captivity.

Equipped with highly developed sensors on its nose, this Blacktip Reef quickly located a fish carcass hidden by the photographer.
Overleaf: A Blacktip Reef cruises the flats in Fakarava, French Polynesia.

The Sentinel of the Deep

We become a bit anxious and restless just thinking about a chance encounter with a Sand Tiger (*Carcharias taurus*) on a deep, dark shipwreck. After all, it personifies our primal fears about sharks, with its dagger-like teeth and cold, sinister stare. Quite simply, for most people, it's the ultimate nightmare.

But for others, it's a dream come true, and it happens in the Outer Banks of North Carolina. Hundreds of shipwrecks litter the ocean's sandy bottom there, including Blackbeard's *Queen Anne's Revenge;* the Union's first iron-clad battleship, the *USS Monitor*; and even a German submarine, the *U-352*, sunk by the US Coast Guard during World War II. Known as the "Graveyard of the Atlantic," the Outer Banks is a region rich in history and wildlife.

The audacious divers braving the choppy seas off the North Carolina coast have nothing to fear, as the Sand Tiger is virtually harmless.

Although large – around 12 ft. – and well equipped to do some serious damage, this species prefers to hang around the wrecks during the day and hunt at night. It's also the only shark known to swallow air from the surface to help it stay neutrally buoyant.

It is very tolerant of divers and is one of the easiest sharks to photograph. Besides North Carolina, the Sand Tiger can be encountered in Australia, South Africa, Lebanon and Japan.

Protected in several countries, it remains extremely endangered.

Brotherly "love": Sand Tiger embryos eat each other before birth and only the strongest two are born.

The entire spectrum of marine life converges on the North Carolina wrecks. *Clockwise from left*: tiny, shiny Cigar Minnows (*Decapterus punctatus*), predatory Almaco Jack (*Seriola rivoliana*) and the non-native Lionfish (*Pterois volitans*)

Diver and Great Hammerhead (*Sphyrna mokarran*); Juno Beach, FL

Diving with Sharks
Frequently Asked Questions

One of the most enjoyable aspects of my work is presenting every year to thousands of school children and introducing them to the wonderful world of sharks. They ask many questions about the toothy predators. Here are some of their favorites:

Have you been attacked?

Once a Grey Reef tried to bite me during a feeding dive. If it weren't for the assistance of a divemaster who beat the shark off with a metal pole, I would have certainly been bitten on the arm or shoulder.

How do you photograph sharks?

The only reliable way to photograph sharks is to lure them in with food. Without it, it would be very difficult to get many images, as they are generally afraid of people.

What are the best places to see sharks?

It depends on the species. Popular locations include Australia, the Bahamas, Florida, Fiji, French Polynesia, Costa Rica, and South Africa for Tigers, Bulls, Whites and the reef sharks.

Tiger shark (*Galeocerdo cuvier*); South Africa

Are you ever afraid?

There were occasions in South Africa that were certainly scary, like swimming with fur seals in Shark Alley, a popular hangout for Great Whites near Capetown, or being alone in the water with five hungry Tigers offshore Durban.

What's your favorite shark?

They're all different and interesting. I like them all, but especially the crafty Blacktip Reef. It's smart and highly unlikely to bite.

Great White Shark (*Carcharodon carcharias*); Mexico

Is the Whale shark a fish or a whale?

The Whale shark is the world's largest fish. We call it "Whale shark" because it can grow larger than many whales, to 40 ft.

Why is the Hammerhead so strange?

Its unusual head is an adaptation, improved over millions of years, that allows it to turn faster and smell better than the other sharks.

Do all sharks have to swim in order to breathe?

Contrary to popular belief, several species can rest motionless and breathe. These include the Bull, Sandbar and Caribbean Reef.

Bull Shark (*Carcharhinus leucas*); Fiji

Whale shark (*Rhincodon typus*); Palm Beach, FL

Swan Song for Sharks?
Devastation in the High Seas

Approximately 70 million sharks, like this Tiger (*Galeocerdo cuvier*) photographed offshore Pacific Harbor, Fiji, are killed every year – for their fins, meat, jaws and leather. They are also killed when fishermen target other fish, like tuna.

Pretty soon, we are going to run out of sharks, plain and simple. They mature slowly and produce only a few young at a time. Their populations just don't have the capacity to replace the millions lost every year. Worldwide, development and pollution also destroy nursing and hunting areas like mangroves and shallow reefs.

The implications of the slaughter are already being felt, in North Carolina, as we examined, and in many other places. The removal of apex predators like sharks creates a negative, cascading effect in the environment.

Part of nature's "clean-up crew," they keep prey populations in check and help maintain the oceans in balance.

So, what can we do to help? Learning about ocean conservation and making sound decisions on how we live and eat are major steps. Through minimal adjustments in our lifestyles, we can reduce our impact on the oceans so they remain healthy and in harmony for future generations.

Batfish Books - Your Passport to Learning & Exploration!

ISBN 978-0-9728653-1-9
$15.95

ISBN 0-9728653-3-0
$15.95

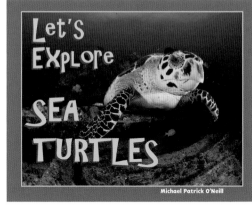

ISBN 0-9728653-2-2
$15.95

ISBN 978-0-9728653-5-7
$19.95

ISBN 978-0-9728653-4-0
$19.95

ISBN 0-9728653-0-6
$19.95

Batfish Books   P.O. Box 32909   Palm Beach Gardens, FL   33420

info@batfishbooks.com   www.batfishbooks.com